Ecology

Donna Latham

www.raintreepublishers.co.uk
Visit our website to find out
more information about
Raintree books.

To order:
☎ Phone 0845 6044371
🖨 Fax +44 (0) 1865 312263
✉ Email myorders@raintreepublishers.co.uk

Customers from outside the UK please telephone +44 1865 312262

Raintree is an imprint of Capstone Global Library Limited,
a company incorporated in England and Wales having
its registered office at 7 Pilgrim Street, London, EC4V 6LB
– Registered company number: 6695582

Edited by Adam Miller, Andrew Farrow, and
 Adrian Vigliano
Designed by Philippa Jenkins and Ken Vail
Original illustrations © Capstone Global Library
 Limited 2009
Illustrated by Gary Joynes pp. 8, 34, 35; Ian Escott
 pp. 11, 13; Maurizio De Angelis pp.15, 17
Picture research by Ruth Blair and Kay Atlwegg
Originated by Raintree
Printed and bound by CTPS (China Translation and Printing
Services Ltd)

ISBN 978 1 406211 54 2 (hardback)
13 12 11 10 09
10 9 8 7 6 5 4 3 2 1

ISBN 978 1 406211 62 7 (paperback)
14 13 12 11 10
10 9 8 7 6 5 4 3 2 1

British Library Cataloguing in Publication Data
Latham, Donna
Ecology. – (Sci-hi)
577-dc22
A full catalogue record for this book is available from the
British Library.

Acknowledgements
The publishers would like to thank the following for
permission to reproduce copyright material: iStockphoto/Rick
Carroll p. **iii** (contents top); iStockphoto/Frank Leung p. **iii**
(contents bottom); Alamy/WorldFoto p. **4**; FLPA/Mitsuaki
Iwago/Minden Pictures p. **5**; FLPA/ p. **7**; SCIENCE PHOTO
LIBRARY/JOHN DURHAM p. **9**; Alamy/blickwinkel p. **10**;
NHPA/Martin Harvey p. **12**; NHPA/Martin Harvey p. **14**; Alamy/
Noella Ballenger p. **17**; Getty Images/Alfred Eisenstaedt;
Time Life Pictures p. **18**; iStockphoto/Frank Leung p. **19**;
SCIENCE PHOTO LIBRARY/JOHN MITCHELL p. **20**; Photos
by Clay DeGayner p. **21**; iStockphoto/Tammy Peluso p. **22**;
iStockphoto/ p. **23**; naturepl.com/Kim Taylor p. **25**; naturepl.
com/Simon King p. **26**; iStockphoto/ p. **27**; iStockphoto/Roger
Whiteway p. **28**; NHPA/Stephen Dalton p. **29**; FLPA/S & D & K
Maslowski p. **30**; iStockphoto/Rick Carroll p. **31**; iStockphoto/
Govert Nieuwland p. **32**; Art Directors and Trip/Helene Rogers
p. **33**; Reuters/Punit Paranjpe p. **36**; iStockphoto/Pauline
Mills p. **37**; FLPA/Tony Hamblin p. **38**; Shutterstock/Geoff
Delderfield p. **39**; SCIENCE PHOTO LIBRARY/NASA p. **40**;
Shutterstock background images and design features.

Cover photo of an anemonefish in anemone used with
permission of Photolibrary/Carol Buchanan **main**. Cover
image of a dung beetle/scarab beetle used with permission of
Alamy/© Arco Images GmbH **inset**.

The publishers would like to thank literacy consultant
Nancy Harris and content consultant Michael Bright for their
assistance in the preparation of this book.

Every effort has been made to contact copyright holders
of material reproduced in this book. Any omissions will be
rectified in subsequent printings if notice is given to the
publishers.

Contents

What almost killed off the bald eagle?

Go to page 19 to find out!

What is this fox doing in the city?

Turn to page 31 to find out!

Some words are shown in bold, **like this**. These words are explained in the glossary. You will find important information and definitions underlined, <u>like this</u>.

INTERACTION WITH THE ENVIRONMENT

Lounging on a tree limb, a leopard eyes you suspiciously. Cubs huddle in high grasses below her. A herd of zebra thunders across vast grasslands. Above you, on a soaring plateau, a waterfall rushes.

It's taken you a long time to get here, travelling by 4 x 4 through the rainy season. But it's worth the journey! Welcome to Nyika National Park. Spread across about 3,200 square kilometres (1,250 square miles) in Malawi, Africa, it's one of the most spectacular **ecosystems** on Earth.

An ecosystem is a group of living and non-living things. They all live in the same **environment** (natural surroundings). These animals, plants, and **micro-organisms** (tiny **organisms**) are interdependent. They can't live without one another. They constantly interact. They relate with their environment, too. Living and non-living things both affect and are affected by their surroundings.

Nyika National Park is home to central Africa's greatest number of leopards.

In Nyika National Park, scattered shrubs and trees rise over grasses. The endangered zebra is one inhabitant of the national park. Zebras are grazing members of the horse family. How do they depend on their environment? Zebras require plenty of space to roam. They also need a good water source. That's why herds never wander more than 32 kilometres (20 miles) from watering holes.

Zebras also depend on their herds. When predators such as leopards and cheetahs attack one zebra, the herd responds. The herd bunches together and confronts the enemy. They stare down the predator until it runs away.

Zebras need plenty of space to graze for food.

Did you know?

No two people have identical fingerprints, and no two zebras have the exact same pattern of stripes. Scientists believe the unique patterns help zebras identify one another in large herds.

Ecosystems – staying alive

Ecosystems are dynamic. They burst with energy. Their members perform jobs to keep their natural surroundings alive and balanced. <u>A healthy ecosystem includes the components (parts) below. Working together, the parts form a system.</u>

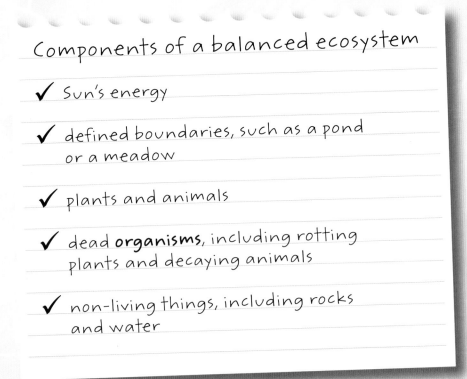

Components of a balanced ecosystem

✓ Sun's energy

✓ defined boundaries, such as a pond or a meadow

✓ plants and animals

✓ dead **organisms**, including rotting plants and decaying animals

✓ non-living things, including rocks and water

Common confusion

Some people confuse the terms biome and ecosystem. A biome is a large geographical area where certain vegetation grows. It features a certain climate and soil. Specific plants and animals inhabit it. For example, the desert is a biome. In contrast, an ecosystem has smaller boundaries. A 15-metre (50-foot) saguaro cactus in New Mexico's Sonora Desert can form the centre of an ecosystem.

A saguaro cactus

A rocky area defines the ecosystem's edge. The scorching Sun, a non-living thing, shines overhead. Yet, a hole in a cool cactus provides a safe place for an elf owl's nest. The owl enjoys a birds-eye view of tasty scorpions below. When the saguaro's flowers bloom, bats, insects, and birds sip sweet nectar. They flit from blossom to blossom and spread pollen. That helps fruit grow. Later, fruit and seeds fall to the ground. Hungry coyotes and pig-like javelinas eat them up. When these animals spread seeds in their dung, more cacti grow.

A saguaro can live for 150 years! When one dies, its pulpy flesh plops to the desert floor. With the help of insects and bacteria, it rots. Decomposed, it becomes part of the desert's gritty soil.

A saguaro cactus can become a home to many animals, including these elf owls.

7

SUNLIGHT AND PHOTOSYNTHESIS

All ecosystems depend on the Sun. Sunlight produces all of Earth's energy. The Sun's energy is called solar energy.

In ecosystems, plants make their own food. They convert solar energy to chemical energy through **photosynthesis**. How? Plants use solar energy from sunlight, water (H_2O) from soil, and carbon dioxide (CO_2) from air. The panel below and the diagram on the right explain how plants combine these three ingredients.

From sunlight to energy

Through roots, plants suck water from the ground. They take in carbon dioxide through **stomata**. Stomata are microscopic **pores** (tiny openings) on the underside of leaves. They open and shut like mouths. Stomata allow water and gases to pass in and out of the plant.

Did you know leaves are a plant's food factories? Inside leaf **cells** (the smallest parts of organisms) are **chloroplasts**. Chloroplasts are tiny solar panels, built to capture sunlight. Inside them is **chlorophyll**, a green **pigment** (colour).

Chloroplasts perform photosynthesis. They turn the three ingredients into **carbohydrates**, such as glucose. Glucose is a simple sugar. Carbohydrates feed the plant. As the first link in the **food chain**, they also fuel animals and people. (You'll learn more about food chains on page 10.)

Plants also **respire** (use energy from food). When plants respire they use oxygen to break down sugar. They release carbon dioxide.

Many of the small dark blobs inside these leaf cells are chloroplasts.

solar energy

oxygen, O_2

chloroplasts

carbon dioxide, CO_2

water, H_2O

stomata

Food chains, food webs, and energy pyramids

A **community** is formed of **organisms** that live and interact in one natural area. <u>**Food chains** show what the members of a community eat.</u>

Producers and consumers

The Sun's energy passes from one organism to another. Plants make their own food through **photosynthesis**. They also become food for animals. Plants are **producers**, the first link in the food chain.

Consumers come next. Consumers are animals that eat producers. For example, chipmunks eat berries. **Herbivores** eat only plant food, including grass and stems. They eat seeds, flowers, fruit, and bark. Grasshoppers, goats, and gorillas are herbivores, as are deer and hippos. **Omnivores** feed on plants and animals. For example, grizzly bears feast on grasses and berries. But they also eat wasps, fish, and goats. Chickens and foxes are omnivores. So are many people.

When herbivores and omnivores eat, the Sun's energy moves up the chain. **Carnivores** reign at the top. These meat-eating predators prey on other animals. Cougars, lions, and sharks are carnivores.

Hippos are herbivores. They wander at night to find plants to eat.

Decomposers

Food chains depend on **decomposers**. Decomposers do an **ecosystem's** dirty work. They eat wastes and devour dead plants and animals. For example, dung beetles collect balls of dung (waste) for food. **Fungi**, bacteria, and insects are decomposers. They break down dead things. Decomposers send nutrients back into the ecosystem through the soil. Then plants absorb the nutrients. The energy stored in the plants transfers along the chain.

Missing from the chain

One part of a food chain depends on another. Imagine an ecosystem with only producers and consumers. Over time, the plants will take all the minerals from the soil. Without minerals, plants will die. A chain reaction will then happen. The herbivores will have nothing to eat. Without plants and herbivores to feed on, the omnivores will starve. Soon, even the big carnivores will die. No longer balanced, the whole ecosystem will collapse.

A savanna food chain

wild dog
(carnivore)

baboon
(omnivore)

grasshopper
(herbivore)

dung beetle
(decomposer)

grass
(producer)

Food webs

A food chain illustrates one path of energy. For example, the chain on page 11 shows a simple path:

Grass → Grasshopper → Baboon → Wild dog

But ecosystems aren't simple. They are made up of a variety of plants and animals. Most animals feast on several foods. So they might be part of several chains.

<u>In a single ecosystem, different food chains share the same food sources.</u> For example, the grasshopper eats grass. Yet, antelopes and wildebeests live in the same ecosystem. They feed on grass, too. In the illustration on page 11 you can see that a wild dog preys on the baboon. Leopards and cheetahs, neighbours in the ecosystem, enjoy the same dinner.

These feeding relationships are complicated. <u>Food webs illustrate the way food chains connect.</u> Like food chains, the energy flow in food webs begins with plants. Study the food web on the right to trace the different paths of energy that flow through it.

In a savanna food web, a dead herbivore provides food for several different animals.

A savanna food web

The LION is the top carnivore.

Did you know?

Vultures are scavengers. They eat dead animals. Vultures do not carry chunks of meat back to their nests to feed their young. Instead, they **regurgitate**. They bring up partially digested food from their stomachs. Then they pour the hot meal into their babies' mouths.

The WILD DOG eats the wildebeest, antelope, and the baboon.

WILDEBEEST

ANTELOPE

The BABOON eats the grasshopper and the grass.

GRASSHOPPER

GRASS is the food source for the wildebeest, antelope, grasshopper, and baboon.

DUNG BEETLES are decomposers that break down dead organisms.

DEAD ORGANISM

Biomass and energy pyramids

Biomass is organic (living) material. It can grow, be used, and then grow again. Plant biomass is produced by a process called photosynthesis. Biomass contains stored energy from the Sun. When herbivores eat plants, they store some of this energy and their own biomass increases.

An energy pyramid shows the energy levels in an ecosystem. Each level shows how energy flows when one type of organism eats another. Study the pyramid on page 15. Notice that the levels get smaller as they move up. That's because the energy flow decreases as it passes along a food chain.

The bottom level of an energy pyramid is the largest. It contains plant biomass from producers. You know plants use the Sun's energy to grow. They store some energy. That energy is used by the herbivores at the second level. When herbivores like giraffes and antelopes munch plants, they consume the energy. Some energy gets stored in their bodies as fat and meat. Most is used right away for grazing, dodging predators, and staying warm. At the top of this pyramid is a lion. There is less energy at the top of the pyramid, so there are fewer top carnivores.

In the savanna, a fierce lion eats and gets energy from a plant-eating antelope.

Design an energy pyramid

Choose an ecosystem, such as a pond, a bog (area with wet, muddy ground), or a forest. Research the types of producers and consumers that live there. Then design an energy pyramid that shows how specific producers and consumers pass energy. Look at the energy pyramid below as an example.

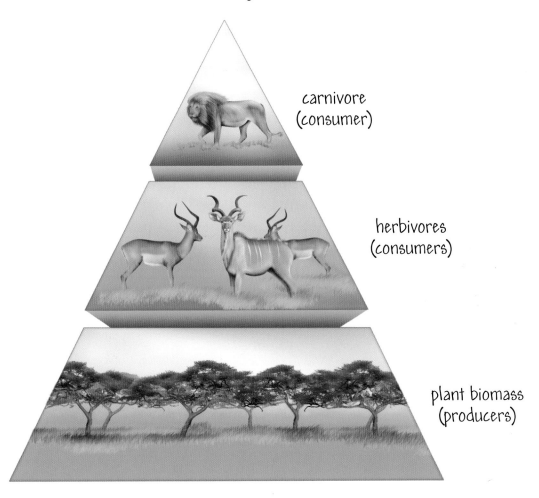

Savanna energy pyramid

carnivore
(consumer)

herbivores
(consumers)

plant biomass
(producers)

BIOMAGNIFICATION

What happens when a dangerous substance enters the food chain? It increases at each level. This process is called **biomagnification**. Let's look at an example.

Spraying pesticide

In the 1950s, pesky insects invaded fruit orchards. Valuable crops suffered. Crop dusters took to the skies. The small planes contained spraying systems in their wings. The dusters dipped over the trees. They sprayed new **pesticides**, chemicals that kill insects.

Pesticides move up the chain

Eventually, rainstorms swept over the sprayed orchards. The water ran off and carried pesticide with it. It drained into rivers, which flowed into the oceans. The pesticide contaminated (polluted) the oceans. Next, green algae in the water took in the pesticide. Algae are a group of simple plants that do not produce flowers.

When small fish ate the algae, pesticide entered their bodies. It added to the pesticide levels the fish had already taken in. The stored pesticide grew stronger or more concentrated. Soon, seagulls gulped down the fish. A higher concentration of pesticide entered the gulls. In this way, pesticide moved up the food chain.

On a rocky ledge beside an ocean, a peregrine falcon swept down. In mid-air, it captured a seagull in its sharp talons. It ate the prey. Now, highly concentrated pesticide moved to the top of the food chain.

Pesticide doesn't kill a falcon. However, it harms the calcium in the bird's body. Falcons need calcium for healthy eggs. When they lay eggs, they are fragile. They crack under a nesting falcon's weight. So fewer baby falcons were born, and peregrine falcon numbers fell.

BIOMAGNIFICATION

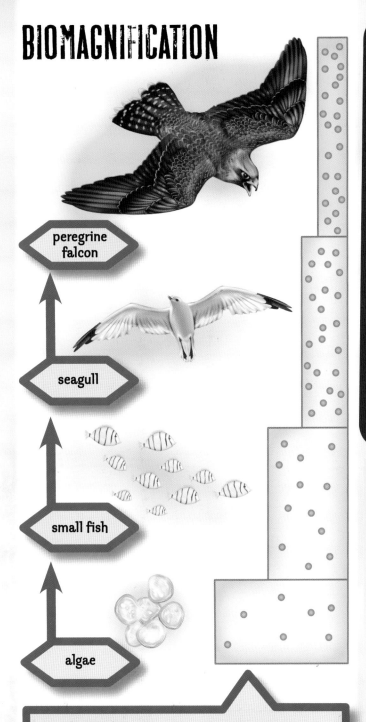

peregrine
falcon

seagull

small fish

algae

A harmful substance can be dangerous to an animal if the animal comes into contact with it. But the same substance can be much more dangerous if that same animal eats another animal that has been exposed to the substance. This happens because of the way animals store substances in their fat.

Did you know?

The word *peregrine* comes from the Latin word *peregrinus*, which means "wanderer". These birds of prey live in every continent but Antarctica.

Other dangers

Many dangerous substances can enter food chains.

◎ Dioxins are dangerous poisons produced as waste when things such as paper are made

◎ Mercury is a very poisonous metal that is used in batteries and **electronics**

◎ Radioactive waste is waste that is contaminated with radiation from nuclear reactions.

Rachel Carson
Ahead of her time

Rachel Carson was a renowned writer and **ecologist**. Born in 1907 in Pennsylvania, USA, she loved nature from an early age. She made the natural world her life's work.

Carson attended the Woods Hole Marine Biology Lab in Cape Cod, Massachusetts, USA. Later, she earned a Master's degree in zoology (the scientific study of animals). A talented writer, Carson penned radio scripts about natural history. She published poetic books about oceans. She suggested that people were part of nature and held power to change it – and not always for the better.

Silent Spring

Carson grew alarmed at the increased use of pesticides, especially the chemical DDT. She studied research about DDT and noted its effect on bald eagle eggs. They became thin-shelled and fragile. Carson warned that when pesticides pass through ecosystems, they affect all its members. In 1962, she published the book *Silent Spring*. She cautioned people that their actions created trouble for other living things.

Carson's research impacted scientific thought. Her writings launched the environmental movement. This is now made up of people and groups around the world who work to protect the environment. Rachel Carson affected the environment itself. Thanks to her efforts, in 1972 the United States government banned the use of DDT. In 1984, the United Kingdom banned DDT. Today, however, the pesticide is still used in some areas of the world.

Did you know?

In 1782, 75,000 bald eagles soared in the United States. By the 1960s, only 900 remained. In 2007, the population had rebounded to 9,789. Scientists believe this increase is directly related to the banning of DDT. Now the majestic eagles have flown off the endangered species list.

Female bald eagles only lay about two to three eggs in a year. Because of this, the species almost died out due to the egg-weakening effects of DDT in the food chain.

Wanted for trespassing – Burmese pythons. One of Earth's largest snakes, these gigantic constrictors can weigh 115 kilograms (250 pounds). They stretch to 6 metres (20 feet). About ten years ago, this huge reptile began to live in the Florida Everglades in the United States. An **invasive species**, the python is creating trouble in the **ecosystem**.

What's an invasive species?

<u>An invasive species is not naturally found in a certain habitat.</u> Burmese pythons' typical home is Asia, in Burma, China, Thailand, and Vietnam. Excellent swimmers, they thrive near water. They eat birds, mammals, lizards, and frogs. In the USA, people kept the pythons as pets. When the pythons grew too large, people released them into the Everglades.

The snakes have proved highly adaptable. They've made themselves at home in the Florida Everglades. There, the pythons have found new foods, such as Kay Largo woodrats, which are endangered animals, and rare round-tailed muskrats. The pythons even battle alligators.

Because there are so many of them in the wild, pythons are now considered to be the main predator in the Everglades.

Animals in the Everglades, such as this endangered Key Largo woodrat, could be easily wiped out if the python problem continues.

Biologists are concerned by threats to protected animals. They also worry the pythons might harm humans. What's more, biologists know that people are still releasing pythons into the Everglades.

Eyes and Ears Team

Now, the problem is spreading. In 2007, researchers noticed that the Burmese python had invaded a new area. Pythons have spread to the Florida Keys. The Keys is a chain of islands that are about 10 kilometres (6 miles) from the Everglades.

Conservationists are working to halt the new invasion. They have contacted local workers, including postal drivers, safety officers, and gardening crews, and asked for help. Now, these workers are part of a special Eyes and Ears Team trained to spot the invading pythons. When they see a python, they call a hotline at the sheriff's office and wait near the snake. Meanwhile, the sheriff's office sends a handler to to safely capture and remove the invader.

So far, it's working. But conservationists worry the invaders could swim to a new location.

Symbiosis

You've learned **ecosystems** burst with energy. Inhabitants interact and interconnect, especially through feeding patterns. **Symbiosis** is another way **organisms** connect. <u>Symbiosis occurs when two different species form relationships. Sometimes these relationships create mutual benefits.</u>

Mutualism

<u>**Mutualism** is a form of symbiosis. In this kind of relationship both species gain something.</u> The clown fish and the sea anemone share this kind of relationship. Both make their homes in saltwater coral reefs. Their partnership keeps both nourished and safe from enemies.

The anemone looks like an underwater flower. A member of the coral family, it's actually an animal. The anemone stings and paralyzes (stuns) prey with poisonous tentacles (a kind of flexible limb). Then, the tentacles stuff motionless prey into an eager mouth.

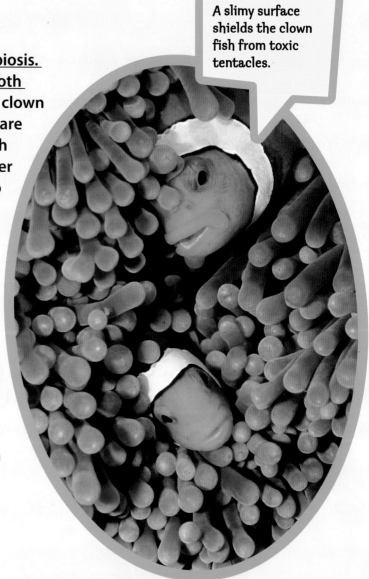

A slimy surface shields the clown fish from toxic tentacles.

A clown fish lives fearlessly between the anemone's toxic tentacles. How? A slippery layer of mucus (a kind of slime made by the fish's body) coats the orange-and-white fish's body.

Mucus protects the clown fish from stings. The lively fish darts in and around the anemone. Its bright colour and movements attract other fish, which the anemone stings and devours.

Clown fish are actually very **aggressive**. If another fish tries to prey on the anemone, the clown fish chases it. The clown fish not only receives a safe home in exchange for luring dinner to the anemone. It also gets the leftovers!

Did you know?

Clown fish are also called anemone fish. Clown fish usually live with mates. There's enough room for two in an anemone.

OTHER SYMBIOTIC RELATIONSHIPS

Research these odd partners to learn more about symbiosis:
◎ Dung beetles and skunk cabbage
◎ Egyptian plover and crocodile
◎ Oxpecker and impala

As part of a symbiotic relationship, impalas allow oxpecker birds to search their bodies for food. Oxpeckers will eat ticks and other parasites right off the impala's body. The oxpeckers get food and the impala has fewer pests!

Parasitism

Parasitism is a form of symbiosis. In a parasitic relationship, only one species benefits. The other suffers. It becomes weak, injured, or ill.

Parasitic relationships involve a parasite, a plant or animal that lives off a host. Imagine you take a dog for a walk in a wooded ecosystem. A flea, so tiny you don't see it, leaps off a shrub. The insect hops onto your dog. First, it sucks blood from the unwilling host. Then, the pesky parasite hitches a ride on the dog as you return home. Within weeks, the flea's offspring latch onto the poor dog, too. Fortunately, you notice the pup's persistent itching. You visit the vet before fleas cause anaemia, a condition that causes too few red blood cells to be produced.

Leeches and flukes

- Along with fleas, ticks and leeches cling to the outside of hosts. Leeches float in marshes and ponds. To feed, leeches latch onto fish, turtles, frogs, and people. With three sets of jaws, leeches gorge on blood and tissue.

- Other parasites, such as flukes and tapeworms, live inside hosts' organs. Flukes thrive in rainforest, forest, and grassland ecosystems. When they enter mammal hosts, flukes settle in the liver. They destroy tissue. Flukes cause liver rot, a disease that wipes out grazing sheep and cows.

Did you know?

Fleas duck their heads and tighten their bodies before hopping. They propel themselves with brawny hind legs. These wingless wonders can leap about 20 centimetres (8 inches) high and 38 centimetres (15 inches) long, which is nearly 200 times their own height! That's like an adult person jumping 37 metres (120 feet)!

Parasites, like this tick which is latched onto a larger animal's head, are typically smaller than their hosts.

Filling a niche

You've learned **ecosystems** must remain balanced to survive. Each species in a **community** plays a certain role that contributes to the system to keep it balanced. This role is a **niche**. In an ecosystem, every species fills a niche.

Niches involve where species live, their feeding relationships, and their **foraging** habits (their searches to find food). Niches also include special activities that species engage in. Visit the Kalahari Desert in Botswana. Observe in action the busy meerkat. Through building and food-finding habits, the meerkat fills its niche.

A clan of meerkats usually numbers about 20. However, some clans have been known to have 50 or more members!

Meerkat niche stats

Description:
Small, ground-dwelling member of the mongoose family

Where it lives:
In **burrows** in the Kalahari Desert, Africa

What it eats:
Carnivorous predator that eats eggs, spiders, lizards, and scorpions

Habits:
Builds burrows to escape heat and predators

Tunnelling through soil, meerkats prevent soil erosion. Precious rainwater collects in burrows.

The Kalahari Desert

The Kalahari is a hostile environment. Rainfall is scarce, only 50 millimetres (2 inches) a year. Temperatures soar to 45 °C (113 °F). Large predators, lions, leopards, and cheetahs, reign at the top of the food chain. Cobras, raptors, and hyenas prey on reptiles, birds, rodents, and insects.

"Little earth men"

Meerkats face predators from sky and land. Hawks, eagles, and jackals are enemies. Sand provides a safer, cooler place to live. The German word for meerkats means "little earth men". These digging mammals create burrows (underground tunnels) in sandy soil.

Meerkats shovel through the soil with long claws. This helps seeds spread. Meerkats loosen the ground. They allow air to reach plant roots.

Meerkats aren't fussy. They eat eggs, insects, spiders, and lizards – just about anything on the Kalahari's menu. Meerkats must carefully unearth and catch their favourite treat, stinging scorpions. They also enjoy juicy insects that gnaw through roots. They eat locusts, ants, and termites that damage plants.

COMPETITION

A pair of 136-kilogram (300-pound) red stags lock antlers. The stags fight over potential mates. An enormous old oak tree stretches high. It snatches sunlight away from a seedling, which withers and dies. A grey squirrel stashes nuts under a log. It conceals others inside a shrub and buries more at the base of a stump. With more than one food-hiding place, the squirrel prevents a chipmunk from stealing all of its food.

Species compete

In **ecosystems**, species compete for food, water, sunlight, and mates. Hawks, eagles, and jackals, for example, compete for meerkats in the Kalahari. **Competition** is the struggle for survival between species for the same limited resources. Competition occurs within species, as it does with the stags battling for mates. Competition over food takes place between different species, like the squirrel and chipmunk.

Red deer stags battle for a mate.

Competition changes ecosystems

Competition can cause changes in ecosystems. In 2007, scientists conducted a study in Antarctica. They noted fur seals and macaroni penguins competed for the same food, krill. Both species dove deep in the waters to hunt for the shrimp-like creature. Gradually, the seal population grew. Seals consumed greater amounts of krill. Competition increased, and the seals gained the upper hand (or flipper)! With less to eat, the penguin population decreased.

Squirrels store seeds and nuts for the winter by hiding them in many small hiding places. Some scientists think that natural competition may sometimes cause squirrels to steal the stored food of other squirrels!

Roaming racoons

As people doze in parts of the United States, **nocturnal** looters prowl around. They topple a rubbish bin. They swarm inside to steal the contents. A band of burglars? No, it's a gaze, a group of racoons.

Increasing trouble

One evening, a person sets out a plate of scraps for the racoons. The next night, the racoons come back with a few pals. Soon, over 20 hungry racoons swarm the neighbourhood every night. They rip open window screens with razor-sharp claws. They climb into attics and squeeze under porches to snooze during the days.

In the wild, racoons thrive in wooded areas near water. Racoons are skilled swimmers and spectacular climbers. They can scramble up tall trees and descend headfirst as they search for shelter and food.

Racoons are not fussy eaters. They are **omnivores**. They hunt small rodents, frogs, and crayfish. They steal duck and turtle eggs from nests, claw worms from the ground, and eat berries and nuts.

When a natural habitat shrinks or vanishes, racoons scavenge for food in urban areas.

Changed ecosystems

Human activity changes natural ecosystems. People clear wooded areas to build homes and businesses. Then, racoons and other wildlife invade urban areas.

Clever and resourceful, racoons adapt quickly to a new environment.

They scavenge for food at night and discover easy pickings in skips and rubbish bins. Racoons feast on items unheard of in the wild. They devour pepperoni pizza and nachos!

Did you know?

Racoons dunk food in water before eating it. Some scientists have suggested racoons do this to soften the food. Scientists think that dunking clears out stones, twigs, and other inedible bits.

URBAN FOXES

It's not just racoons that roam into urban areas when habitats change. In many European cities, people report city foxes trotting across pedestrian crossings and rummaging through rubbish bins.

Foxes in Britain became pests after World War I. New suburbs were springing up around cities and towns. They were built on land where the foxes once lived. The foxes soon got used to feeding on food waste left by humans.

Red foxes have been able to adapt to changing natural habitats. Cities in several continents around the world are seeing red fox populations rise. They survive by eating everything from rats to rubbish!

ECOLOGICAL SUCCESSION

Ecosystems are dynamic. They change constantly. As older **organisms** die, younger ones replace them. Some species die off completely. New species take hold in their place. **Ecological succession is the series of changes in communities** that occurs over time.

Changes in communities

You may have seen news stories about wildfires that wipe out forests. Or about hurricanes that hit coastal regions. Some changes in ecosystems occur because of these natural disasters. Human interference causes other changes. People slash and burn rainforests to clear land for farming. Disastrous oil spills smother coral reefs. Other human-made changes, such as overfishing (taking too many fish from a body of water), change ecosystems, too.

A violent act of nature

Visit southern Europe to witness a violent act of nature. Sicily's Mount Etna rumbles. The volcano, over 3,000 metres (10,000 feet) high, erupts often. It spews fountains of molten rock. It blasts ash and toxic gases. Tongues of lava flow down the mountain. They scorch pine trees that grow nowhere else in Europe.

Mount Etna is one of the world's most active volcanoes. It is the largest active volcano in Europe..

For weeks, tremendous amounts of volcanic ash shower the ecosystem. Ash smothers plants, which can't capture sunlight. Olive crops shrivel. Lingering fires burn beech trees. Over 250 hectares (620 acres) of pine trees burn away.

This natural event can wreck an ecosystem. However, through the wonders of ecological succession, a new one can take its place. Turn the page to find out more!

Did you know?

The ancient Greeks believed the one-eyed creature Cyclops lived in a cave at the base of Mount Etna. In old tales, Cyclops was a powerful giant with a single eye in the middle of its forehead.

This woodcut of Mount Etna erupting was made in 1669!

A Prospect of MOUNT ÆTNA, with its Irruption in 1669.
A Top of Ætna. B Irruption. C Two Hills made by the Irruption. D Fiery Currents. E The Arch of Marcellus. F City of Catania.
1 Montpileri. 2 La Guardia. 3 La Annunciata. 4 La Potielli. 5 Malpasso. 6 Campo Rotundo. 7 St Pietro. 8 St Antonino. 9 Mostorbianco.
10 Falicchi. 11 Placchi. These Towns were quite Consumed, no Footsteps of them remaining. 12 St Giovanni de Galermo. 13 Mascalucia
hardly ruin'd by the Fiery Inundation. a. Nicolosi, wholly ruin'd by the Earthquake. b. Padara. c. Tre Castagne, ruin'd in part.

Stages of succession

After Mount Etna's eruption, an ecosystem can vanish. Where beech and pine trees once stood, rock, lava, and volcanic ash cover the ground. The grey area appears barren. It is quiet, without singing birds and buzzing insects. However, over time, vegetation spreads. In stages, the area transforms, like the stages of succession shown here.

STAGE ❶ Pioneers

You've probably read about brave pioneers. Pioneers ventured into unfamiliar territories. When they explored and found new areas, new farms and towns grew up. Plant pioneers start growth, too. Pioneers are the first plant species to return to a disrupted area. First, **lichens** (simple plants formed from algae and fungi) and mosses cover the ground. Short tufts of grass spring up. Birds, insects, and worms return. Worms plough beneath soil, which becomes more fertile. Birds pluck worms from grasses and disperse the seeds.

STAGE ❷
Herbaceous plants

Pioneers die. Decaying remains add nutrients to the soil. Now, ferns, weeds, and shrubs appear. Low to the ground, they grow in clumps. With more food available, small mammals and more birds settle in the area. Roaming, the mammals scatter seeds through their faeces.

STAGE ❸ Small trees

With richer soil available, small trees, such as pines, take root. They compete for sunlight – and win. Their growth blocks sunlight from shrubs. Some shrubs wither. Their decay fills the soil with more nutrients. Larger birds, including owls and hawks, move in. Foxes, weasels, and wildcats find plenty of prey among dormouse, mouse, and rabbit populations.

STAGE ❹
Climax

Climax is the final stage. Now, birches, beeches, and oaks stand tall. In competition for sunlight, they grew high above small trees. It has taken many years. Yet, in its final stage, the ecosystem is healthy and balanced.

Extinction: gone forever

Through **ecological succession** in a particular area, species come and go. Acts of nature, such as volcanoes and tsunamis (huge sea waves), kill them. Sometimes species vanish through human interference.

As they do in other places in the world, deer, wolves, and wild boars once roamed forests around Mt. Etna. As human populations increased, a greater need for homes developed. People cleared away trees to create space and building materials. Without homes and food, deer, wolves, and boars fled the **ecosystem**. Fortunately, they migrated to other areas, where they thrived.

What happens when a habitat is completely destroyed? Some species become extinct. <u>When a species is extinct, it no longer exists.</u> It's gone forever. Here are some examples of extinction's causes.

Disasters such as the Indian Ocean tsunami of 2004 cause massive destruction. The most lethal geological event in history, the tsunami killed 220,000 people. Huge waves also swept away the eggs of endangered sea turtles, drawing them closer to extinction.

WHAT CAUSES EXTINCTION?

✓ **Climate change** Higher temperatures cause Arctic ice to thin. Without ice to perch on, polar bears can't hunt for seals. The polar bear population has shrunk. In addition, seals and walruses, which share the ecosystem, are at risk.

✓ **Excessive hunting and trapping** Some people kill great numbers of animals for meat, fur, shells, or skin. Have you heard of the dodo? The dodo once lived on the island of Mauritius in the Indian Ocean. When European explorers visited the island in the late 16th century, they over-hunted the turkey-sized bird and caused its extinction. In modern times, Asia's snow leopard has been over-hunted.

✓ **Geological events** Natural occurrences such as earthquakes, extreme floods, and mudslides wipe out species. Widespread extinction occurred 65 million years ago, for example. Some scientists believe a huge **meteor** (falling matter from space) crashed into Earth. This event, combined with other natural disasters like volcanic eruptions, may have helped kill the dinosaurs.

✓ **Habitat destruction** People destroy ecosystems through logging, mining, pollution, and **deforestation**. In Borneo, people have cleared forests to make way for palm oil plantations. They have destroyed the endangered orang-utan's habitat.

✓ **Invasive species** Tree snakes invaded the Pacific island of Guam after World War II. How? They hid on ships from their native islands. In their new habitat, tree snakes preyed on Guam's reptiles. They devoured the island's birds, and several species became extinct. (The invaders caused massive power cuts, too. They slithered up power poles and across electrical lines.)

Higher temperatures have melted the ice platforms polar bears use to hunt on. Polar bear populations are lower as a result.

Protecting endangered species

<u>Laws protect endangered species.</u> You've learned bald eagles soared off the endangered species list in 2007. After the United States government banned DDT in the 1970s, eagles' eggs gradually grew less fragile. The eagle population slowly increased. In the UK during the 1960s, the sparrowhawk population declined. Why? The predators devoured prey that had been contaminated with DDT and other pesticides. Sparrowhawks produced eggs with thin shells. Fortunately, after the government banned DDT in the 1980s, sparrowhawk populations grew again.

Organizations comprised of concerned people work to protect and preserve endangered species and their habitats. In 2004, the United Kingdom's People's Trust for Endangered Species sounded an alarm about the Scottish wildcat.

Purebred Scottish wildcats are on the brink of extinction.

Scottish wildcats

At one time, wildcats prowled much of Britain. The population diminished through habitat destruction. Feral cats, once raised as pets but released in the wild, pose another threat. They mate with wildcats and create **hybrids**. Hybrids are a mix between wildcat and feral cat. Today, fewer than 400 purebred wildcats remain. They live only in the Scottish Highlands.

Ferocious predators resemble pets

Scottish wildcats resemble tabby cats, one of the world's most popular pets. Both have striped bodies and bushy, ringed tails with black tips. Yet, the tabby is **domesticated**. It's accustomed to sharing a life with people. The wildcat, however, is a fierce predator. Some scientists believe the cat, even raised in captivity, is completely untamable.

Tabby cats closely resemble the wildcat.

Research an endangered animal

- Select one or more of the following endangered animals: bobcat, killer whale, manatee, panda bear, leatherback sea turtle, macaw, gorilla, kiwi.

- Next, use print and online sources to find out about the animal and why it's endangered.

- Then, copy and complete the chart to share your findings.

Animal	Where it lives	Why it's endangered	How people are helping

Did you know?

Over 1,900 years ago, ancient Romans first introduced domesticated cats to Britain.

The Roman army kept cats as good luck charms. When the cats arrived in Britain, they mated with wildcats. Later, when the Roman army departed, they left their cats behind. People took the strays into their homes as pets.

Pollution: you can help

Ecosystems are interconnected. When changes occur in one area, the entire system responds. Pollution disrupts and damages ecosystems.

This satellite image shows the lights of Europe at night. Light pollution impacts many plants and animals by changing their environment. These effects are felt throughout the ecosystem, from night-blooming flowers, plankton, and moths, to migrating birds, frogs, and salamanders.

Types of pollution

- **Air pollution** Car exhausts, cigarette smoke, and industrial emissions (substances released from places like factories) pollute our air. Burning fuels release carbon dioxide gas, which contributes to **global warming**.

- **Light pollution** Streetlights and flashing neon signs cast an artificial glow. Light pollution doesn't just obstruct your view of stars. It confuses wildlife, especially migratory birds. Some depend on stars to find their way.

- **Land pollution** People destroy ecosystems through **deforestation**, logging, and **mining**. They dump rubbish, everything from paper to rusty bikes, in landfills.

- **Water pollution** A person tosses a plastic bottle in a lake. A factory dumps chemicals in a river. A tanker spills oil in the ocean. Human activities pollute water. They destroy **aquatic food chains** and harm drinking water.

CREATE AN OUTDOOR COMPOST

How can you help? Don't add food scraps and garden waste to landfills. Send them back into the soil by **composting** waste! Ask an adult to help.

- Your area may have specific composting regulations. Check first.

- You'll need gardening gloves, a compost bin, newspapers, dry leaves, food scraps, garden waste, water, a thermometre, and a garden fork.

- Protect your hands with the gloves. Add "brown" items to the bin. These sources of carbon include newspapers and dry leaves.

- Add a layer of "green" items. These sources of nitrogen include grass cuttings, apple cores, and eggshells.

- Keep layering browns and greens.

- Moisture and air speed the process. Add water, but don't soak the pile.

- The pile will heat up. After a few days, check it with the thermometre. Is the temperature about 60–70 °C (140–160 °F)?

- Don't add meat or fish to the compost. When they rot they are dangerous, and they'll smell terrible. They will also attract pests.

- With an adult's help, use the grden fork daily to turn the pile. In time, crumbly dark material should develop. This is your compost.

- Thoroughly wash your hands afterwards.

You've learned a balanced **ecosystem** has defined boundaries. It requires the Sun's energy. It's made up of living **organisms**, such as plants and animals, and dead ones, such as decaying animals. Non-living things, including water and rocks, are also part of an ecosystem.

Visit a natural area. Then select an ecosystem to explore. For example, you might choose a school field, a woodland, or the land near a lake or stream. <u>You must have permission from the landowner to dig in certain areas.</u>

You will need:

- Gardening gloves
- A copy of the chart on page 43
- Pen
- Small gardening shovel
- Magnifying glass

Explore

- Select one target area to investigate. You might pick a sunny clearing or a shady corner.
- Study your surroundings. What living things do you observe? What non-living things are present in the area?

Copy and complete the chart

- Note the living and non-living items on the chart.

- Look for a water source. If there is one, describe it on the chart.

- Note the amount of sunlight. Record it on the chart.

- Wear gardening gloves for protection. Use caution when touching items in the ecosystem. Plants can cause **allergic reactions**. They might contain thorns.

- With the spade, dig up a small soil sample.

- With the magnifying glass, examine the soil. Describe the sample on the chart.

Clean up

- Carefully return the soil sample to its original position. Pat it in place with the spade.

- Don't disrupt the ecosystem. Leave everything as you found it.

- Wash your hands thoroughly afterwards.

Sample completed chart

Location	Water source	Level of sunlight	Living things	Non-living things	Soil description
Field next to school	Small pond borders field	Very bright	Rabbits, squirrels, butterflies, bees, flies	Rocks, gravel, sunlight, soil	Moist, rich earth with worms inside

Quiz

Check what you learned by answering these questions.

1 Ecology is the study of relationships between what?
a. parasites and hosts
b. biomes and ecosystems
c. food chains and energy pyramids
d. living things and their environment

2 An ecosystem is a group of interdependent living and non-living things that all live where?
a. in the same environment
b. in the wilderness
c. in parasitic relationships
d. in cities and suburbs

3 The struggle for survival between species for identical resources is what?
a. parasitism
b. succession
c. competition
d. ecosystem

4 Which of the following is an example of air pollution?
a. glaring city lights
b. oil spills
c. industrial emissions
d. deforestation

5 Which of these is an example of an act of nature that impacts an ecosystem?
a. a dust storm that destroys a wheat field
b. a farmer who clears trees so cattle can graze
c. a factory that dumps chemicals in a lake
d. a fire that campers accidentally start on a mountain

Answers on page 47.

Glossary

aggressive likely to attack or confront

allergic reaction physical reaction to a substance

aquatic found in or depending on water

biomagnification process in which a dangerous substance, such as a pesticide, increases at each level of the food chain

biomass renewable organic material, such as grass or leaves

burrow hole or tunnel dug by an animal, often as a home

carbohydrate natural compound that is in living things and many foods. Sugar is a kind of carbohydrate.

carnivore meat-eating animal

cell smallest functioning unit of an organism

chlorophyll green chemical in plants

chloroplast plant organelle in which photosynthesis takes place

community all the living things that live and interact in a natural area

competition struggle for survival between species for the same resources

composting process of decaying organic matter so it can be used as fertilizer

Congress group of people responsible for passing laws in the United States

consumer animal that feeds on producers

decomposer fungi, bacteria, and insects that eat waste and break down nutrients from dead bodies

deforestation process of clearing or cutting down an area of trees or forest

domesticated adapted to life with people

ecologist scientist who studies organisms and how they relate to each other and their environment

ecology study of relationships between living things and their environment

ecosystem group of living and non-living things that live in the same environment and rely on one another for survival

electronics devices that use electricity

environment natural surroundings

food chain line of organisms that depend on one another for survival. Each organism provides food for the next organism in the chain.

forage search for food

fungi group of plant-like organisms that produce spores, such as mushrooms

global warming slow increase in the temperature of Earth's atmosphere, due in part to pollution

herbivore plant-eating animal

hybrid animal that is made when animals from two separate species mate

invasive species plant or animal that is not native to a particular area. They become problems because they eat or take resources from native species.

lichen simple plant formed from algae and fungi

meteor object from space that enters Earth's atmosphere

micro-organism tiny organism

mining digging in the earth to find things such as gold or minerals

mutualism kind of symbiosis in which both creatures gain something from the relationship

niche organism's role in an ecosystem

nocturnal active at night

omnivore animal that eats both plants and animals

organism living thing

parasitism symbiotic relationship in which one species benefits and the other does not

pesticide chemical that kills insects

photosynthesis process in which green plants use energy from the Sun to make their own food

pigment substance that makes colour

pore tiny opening in the skin or surface of an organism

producer basic level of all food chains. Plants are producers.

regurgitate bring swallowed food up again

respire process plants go through to use energy from food. The plants use oxygen to break down sugar.

stomata tiny pores in the outer layers of plants that take in air and allow water to pass through

symbiosis relationship between two species which may be beneficial for only one or both species

terrestrial found on or related to land

Find out more

Books

Eco-Action: Energy of the Future, Angela Royston (Heinemann Library, 2007)

Living Things (series), Robert Snedden (Franklin Watts, 2007)

Making Sense of Science: Life on Earth, Peter Riley (Franklin Watts, 2004)

Why Science Matters: Protecting Threatened Species, Sally Morgan (Heinemann Library, 2009)

Websites

http://www.bbc.co.uk/schools/ks3bitesize/science/biology/feeding_intro.shtml
This site helps you to revise all that you've learnt about feeding relationships.

http://www.wwfus.org/
The World Wildlife Fund exists to protect endangered species and their habitats.

http://www.envirolink.org/
This website provides up-to-date news and information on the environment.

Quiz answers

1. d **2**. a **3**. c **4**. c **5**. a

Index